Discovering Light in Nature

Jill Bryant

Discovering Light in Nature

Text: Jill Bryant
Publishers: Tania Mazzeo and Eliza Webb
Series consultant: Amanda Sutera
Hands on Heads Consulting
Editor: Kirstie Innes-Will
Project editor: Jarrah Moore
Designer: Leigh Ashforth
Project designer: Danielle Maccarone
Diagrams: David Rojas Marquez
Permissions researcher: Lumina Datamatics
Production controller: Renee Tome

Acknowledgements
We would like to thank the following for permission to reproduce copyright material:

Front cover: Fer Gregory/Shutterstock.com; p. 4: fukume/Shutterstock.com; p. 5 (top): Richard A McMillin/Shutterstock.com, (bottom): altanaka/Shutterstock.com; p. 6 (top): angelinast/Adobe Stock Photos, (bottom left), Content page: Stocktrek Images, Inc./Alamy Stock Photo, (bottom right): Tragoolchitr Jittasaiyapan/Shutterstock.com; p. 7 (top): Pawel Papis/Shutterstock.com, (bottom): CHAINFOTO24/Shutterstock.com; p. 8: Elena Schweitzer/Shutterstock.com; p. 9 (top), back cover: iStock.com/rasslava, (bottom): Ralf Lehmann/Shutterstock.com; p. 10: © Cengage; p. 11 (top), p. 1: Rishav-Rajput/Shutterstock.com, (bottom left): MarcelClemens/Shutterstock.com, (bottom right): Alan Dyer/Alamy Stock Photo; p. 12: iStock.com/Blue Planet Studio; pp. 21, 13 (top): iStock.com/Philip Thurston; (bottom) © Cengage; p. 14 (top): Snappy Sammy/Adobe Stock Photos, (bottom): Jerome Mallefet-FNRS/Minden Pictures; p. 15 (top): Ali Majdfar/Moment/Getty Images, (bottom): Nature Picture Library/Alamy Stock Photo; p. 16: Hugh Mitton/Alamy Stock Photo; p. 17 (top): Andrew Newman Nature Pictures/Alamy Stock Photo, (bottom): iStock.com/MarcelStrelow; p. 18: Petar B photography/Shutterstock.com; p. 19 (top): © Cengage, (bottom): Nature Picture Library/Alamy Stock Photo; p. 20: David Shale/Nature Picture Library; p. 21: Neil Bromhall/Shutterstock.com; p. 22: Jennifer Y. Lamb; p. 23 (top): MELVYN YEO/Science Photo Library, (bottom): Borisoff/Shutterstock.com; p. 24 (top): Dominik Rueß/Adobe Stock Photos, (bottom): J. Martin, Northland College; from Anich et al. 2020, Mammalia; p. 25 (top): The Western Australian Museum, (bottom): Juergen & Christine Sohns/Minden Pictures/Nature in Stock; p. 26: Anaredif/Shutterstock.com; p. 27 (top): Lee Rentz/Alamy Stock Photo, (bottom): Travis/Adobe Stock Photos; p. 28 (top): Pascal Kobeh/Nature Picture Library, (bottom): Irina Markova/Shutterstock.com; p. 29: Dr. David Gruber; p. 30: Joe Chen Photography/Moment/Getty Images.

Every effort has been made to trace and acknowledge copyright. However, if any infringement has occurred, the publishers tender their apologies and invite the copyright holders to contact them.

NovaStar

ISBN 978 0 17 033480 8

Cengage Learning Australia
Level 5, 80 Dorcas Street
Southbank VIC 3006 Australia
Phone: 1300 790 853
Email: aust.nelsonprimary@cengage.com

For learning solutions, visit **cengage.com.au**

Printed in China by 1010 Printing International Ltd
1 2 3 4 5 6 7 29 28 27 26 25

Nelson acknowledges the Traditional Owners and Custodians of the lands of all First Nations Peoples. We pay respect to Elders past and present, and extend that respect to all First Nations Peoples today.

Contents

Light Around Us

Light is amazing! It allows us to see things. Without light, our world would be cloaked in darkness.

Here are some interesting facts about light:

- Light moves faster than anything else in the universe. In outer space, light travels at almost 300 million metres per second! When light from the Sun reaches Earth's atmosphere, it slows down slightly. But it still travels faster than a blink of an eye.
- **Light beams** travel in straight lines. They bounce back when they hit a solid object such as a wall. They bend when they pass through water or glass.
- Light comes from different **sources**. These sources can be natural or artificial (made by humans).

The Sun is a natural source of light.

There are even sources of light in the ocean, such as this jellyfish.

- Natural sources of light **emit** their own light. The Sun is the brightest source of light in our galaxy. The stars in the sky are also natural sources of light. But natural sources also include some extraordinary living things, such as insects, reptiles, fish, mammals and plants.
- Artificial sources of light include light bulbs, lit candles and torches.

Now, let's explore! We'll look at things that make light in nature. And we'll check out things that play with light, bending and bouncing it in remarkable ways.

Try This!

Try observing your shadow outside in the morning sun, and then later in the afternoon sun. How are your shadows different? Our shadows are longer in the morning and evening when the Sun is low in the sky, and shorter in the afternoon when the Sun is directly overhead.

Finding Light in the Sky

We can discover light in nature just by looking up.

On a clear night, what can you see in the sky? In the southern hemisphere, stargazers can spot the brilliant star Alpha Centauri, which points towards the Southern Cross **constellation**. In the northern hemisphere, observers might be drawn to the brightness of Polaris (the North Star) and the Big Dipper. These stars and constellations are examples of natural light sources in the night sky.

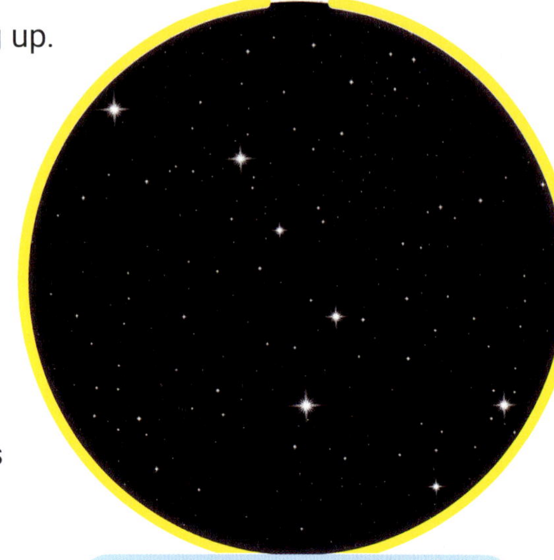

The Big Dipper constellation is a natural source of light.

However, not everything we see in the night sky is a source of light. For example, the Moon and some planets close to Earth appear as strong spots of light in the sky, but they don't produce that light. Instead, the light we see is the Sun's light as it bounces off the surface of the Moon and planets. Awesome!

The planet Venus sometimes looks very bright in the night sky, but it's not a light source.

Alpha Centauri is the third-brightest star in the sky.

Too Much Light

On Earth, lights from houses, streetlights and car headlights make it difficult to see natural light sources in the night sky. This is known as **light pollution.** It's much easier to see the stars in places far away from cities, where there's less artificial light.

On a clear night, away from light pollution, you might see a large band of light across the sky. This is a portion of our galaxy, the Milky Way.

The Sun

The Sun is a star. It's also the most significant natural source of light for all living things on Earth. The Sun is made up of layers of hot gases. These gases are constantly changing. They spin, move wildly and explode outwards. The gases also create **energy**, which streams out in the form of light and heat. Both are essential for life: the Sun's light allows us to see, its heat keeps us warm and its energy helps plants grow.

The Sun's energy allows trees and plants to grow.

The Sun shines its light on half of Earth at a time. This is the half of Earth that is experiencing daytime. The other half is experiencing night-time. Even on cloudy days, light from the Sun makes Earth much brighter than it is at night.

The Sun is far away from Earth. It takes 8 minutes and 20 seconds for the Sun's light to reach us.

The Sun is a natural source of light and heat.

Hot Glow!

"Incandescence" happens when an object gets so hot that it glows with light. The Sun is the best example of incandescence. Other examples of this type of light in nature are hot glowing coals in a fire and hot flowing lava from a volcano.

lava

The Moon and the Planets

Planets such as Mercury, Venus, Mars, Jupiter and Saturn can look bright in the night sky, although we sometimes need special equipment to see them. But the Moon is the largest, brightest object, because it's so close to Earth.

The Moon often looks bright white or bluish. But it doesn't produce light, heat or energy like the Sun does. Instead, the Moon's surface bounces back light from the Sun, just like a mirror. This bouncing back of light is called "reflection".

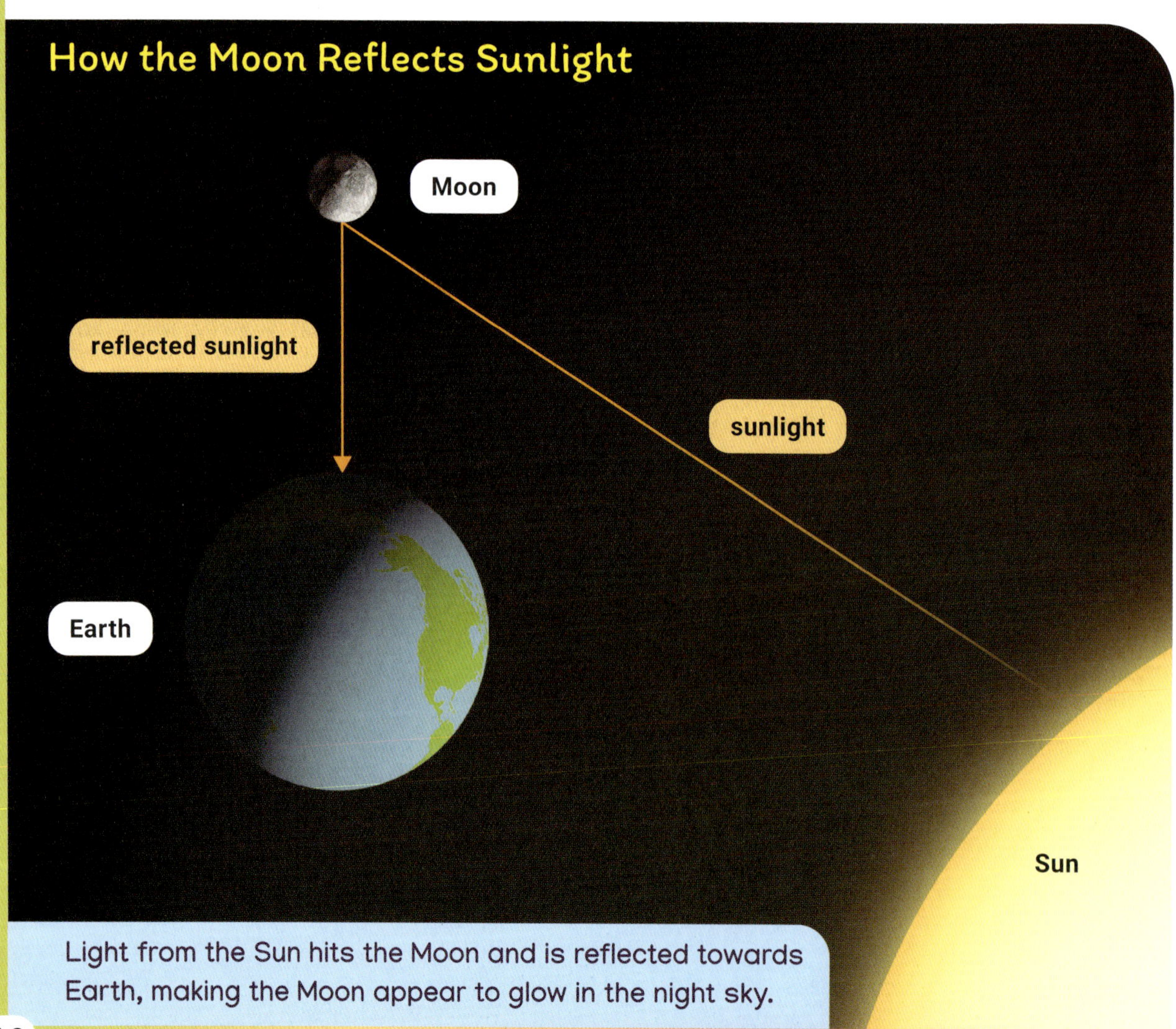

Light from the Sun hits the Moon and is reflected towards Earth, making the Moon appear to glow in the night sky.

The Dark Side

When the Moon looks like a complete circle, it's called a "full" Moon. During this **Moon phase,** reflected light makes it look big and bright. Meanwhile, the other side of the Moon is in darkness, out of reach of the Sun's light (like night and day on Earth).

Venus is often one of the brightest objects in the night sky. This is because it's the closest planet to Earth, and because its surface is covered in thick clouds that reflect the Sun's light.

The surface of Venus is very cloudy.

Venus looks bright because it's near Earth and it reflects the Sun's light.

Rainbows

Let's come back down to Earth. Consider a day when the Sun comes out after a rain shower. Have you ever seen a rainbow stretch across the afternoon sky?

A rainbow is a huge natural arch of light with bands of colour. Rainbows only appear when the conditions are just right. They usually show up during or after a rain shower, when water droplets hang in the air and the Sun is shining.

So, how do rainbows occur? Light shines through the many droplets of water floating in the air. Remember that light beams travel in a straight line. When a beam of light moves from air into water, it slows down slightly and its path bends. The bent beam of light then reflects off the insides of the water droplets.

A white beam of light is actually made up of many different colours, and the colours bend at different angles. This bending of light is called **refraction**.

As the light exits the water drop, the beam bends, or refracts, again. The different colours of light fan out into a brilliant rainbow.

A rainbow isn't a source of light – it is the Sun's light bent into different colours.

Rainbow Colours

From top to bottom, the colours of a rainbow are red, orange, yellow, green, blue, indigo and violet, or dark purple. Between coloured bands, the different shades blend together.

How Sunlight Refracts in Water Droplets

Sun

refraction

sunlight

reflection

water droplet

refraction

When a beam of sunlight enters a droplet of water, it refracts into separate colours, reflects off the inside of the water droplet then refracts again as it leaves the droplet, creating rainbow colours.

Bioluminescent Beings

Where else can we find light? In the animal and plant worlds, of course!

Some amazing living things can emit their own light. This is known as **bioluminescence** (pronounced *bye-oh-loom-in-ess-ence*). A **chemical reaction** takes place in their bodies and gives off light.

Biolumínescence appears in many sea creatures and can appear in plants, birds, insects and reptiles, and other living things too. Bioluminescent creatures and plants exist all around the world. They live in many different places, from sunless caves and lush forests to the deepest parts of the ocean.

Living things give off light for many possible reasons: to attract a **mate**, to capture prey or to protect themselves. Every day, scientists are learning more about bioluminescence.

viperfish

A Healthy Glow: Coral

Corals are plant-like animals that attach themselves to the ocean floor, creating hard or soft structures. They can look like branches, mushrooms, flowers and fans. Many corals are also bioluminescent, emitting their own light.

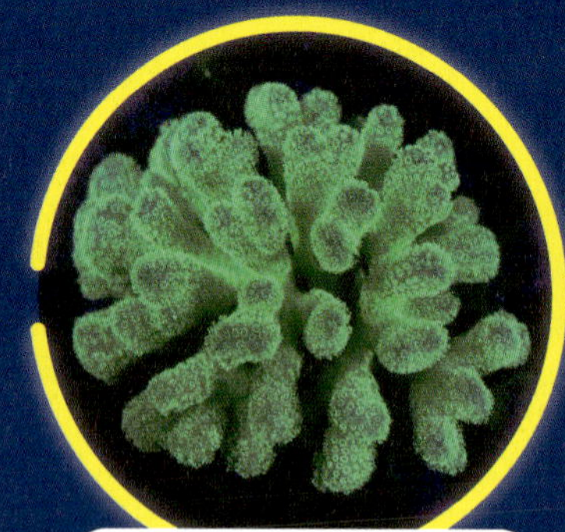

bioluminescent coral

In shallow water, **proteins** in coral absorb sunlight. Then a chemical reaction changes the protein into a green glow that acts like a layer of sunscreen over the coral. The glow helps to protect coral from warming waters and pollution.

Fireflies

One example of a bioluminescent animal is the firefly, a winged beetle. Across North America, people can see fireflies on hot summer evenings in parks, backyards and fields. A chemical reaction makes the firefly's abdomen give off flashes of light.

firefly

A firefly's flash of light has a purpose: to attract a mate. Male fireflies flash in a certain pattern, and an interested female can light up to show her location. After an exchange of light flashes, the pair finds each other.

Fireflies' bright flashes can also be a warning to predators to stay away.

Different kinds of fireflies are found around the world. In some parts of Australia, fireflies can be seen in the spring.

Fireflies create a beautiful glow at night-time with their flashing lights.

Glow-Worms

We can find natural sources of light even in the darkest caves.

The fungus gnat is an insect found in Australia and New Zealand. The larva, or worm-like young, of the fungus gnat glow! They are called glow-worms, even though they are not worms at all.

Glow-worms grow to be about 3 centimetres long, and they are bioluminescent. They produce a blue or green shimmery light. This is caused by a chemical reaction inside a special **organ** near their tails.

Moist environments are the ideal habitat for glow-worms. Although they're most often found inside caves, glow-worms also live in forests where the air is wet and warm.

Glow-worms make strings of silk with their bodies. Then they leave droplets of slimy **mucus** along the silk strings. This makes a sticky trap to catch mosquitoes and tiny flies. The strings are lit by the gleam of the glow-worms' bodies, which attracts the insects. They mistake the light of the glow-worms for the sky, and they are trapped!

The sticky silk threads of glow-worms look like tiny strings of pearls.

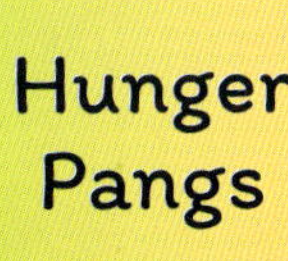

Hunger Pangs

Did you know that the hungrier a glow-worm gets, the brighter the light it emits? And, of course, the bright light attracts insects, which fly toward the light and get trapped and eaten. As the glow-worm eats and becomes less hungry, its light fades.

Glow-worms emit light to catch prey.

Glow-worms emit bright lights in the Waipu Caves, New Zealand.

Ghost Mushrooms

Ghost mushrooms live in damp forests. Found across southern Australia and in some places in India, ghost mushrooms often grow on dead trees, stumps or fallen logs. Bioluminescence allows the mushrooms to emit green light. The process is similar to what happens in the bodies of glow-worms and fireflies.

Ghost mushrooms give off a spooky glow.

Ghost mushrooms look a lot like another type of mushroom called an oyster mushroom, but ghost mushrooms are poisonous. They are shaped like nests or small bowls. Some are cream-coloured, while others are darker shades of brown, orange, grey and purple. The lighter-coloured mushrooms give off the most light, with all parts of the mushroom glowing green: stem, cap and gills.

Some scientists think that certain kinds of mushrooms glow to attract insects. When insects crawl or fly around mushrooms, they help to spread the mushrooms' dust-like spores. Spores are like seeds that help the mushrooms grow in new places.

Parts of a Ghost Mushroom

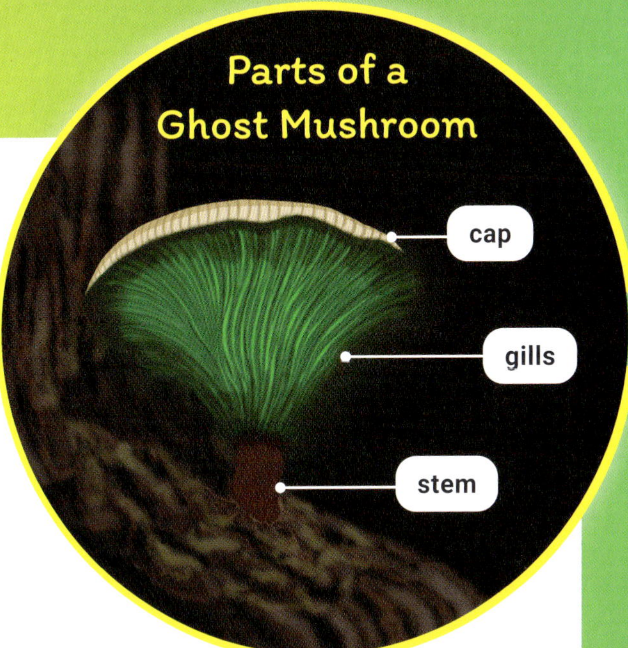

Ghostly Glow

Ghost mushrooms always emit a soft green glow, even in the daytime. But night is the best time to observe the brightest glow, away from other light sources.

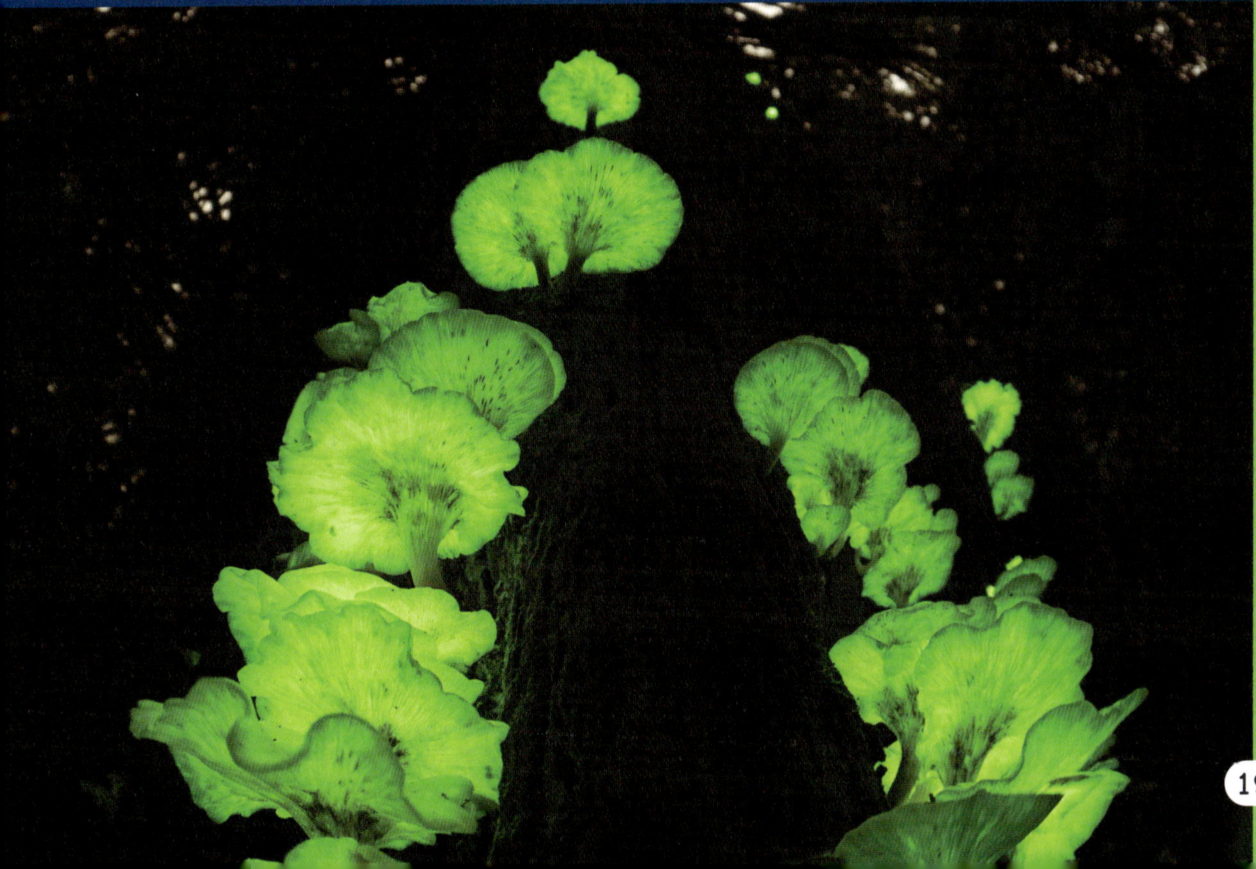

Deep-Sea Anglerfish

Even underwater where it's very cold and completely dark, we can still find sources of natural light.

Deep-sea anglerfish can live at depths of up to 5000 metres below the sea. Female anglerfish use bioluminescence to hunt prey. They have a unique feature: dangling on the end of a long fin sticking out of their back is an organ called an "esca". The esca is coated in **bacteria**, and this bacteria glows in the dark. It can emit a blue-green, yellow-green, orange or bright yellow light.

The esca is used to attract mates as well as to find prey. It hangs in front of the anglerfish's fangs like a **lure** on the end of a fishing rod. The anglerfish jiggles the lure, drawing prey closer. Then it opens its jaws and eats.

To survive in the cold water with few sources of food, anglerfish hide and limit their movement. This helps them save the energy they need to catch food when a squid or fish approaches.

Female anglerfish are between the size of a cricket ball and a volleyball, and they often live more than 300 metres down in the cold, dark, deep ocean.

A Mate for Life!

Male anglerfish are much smaller than females and don't have an esca. In some kinds of anglerfish, six or more males can attach themselves to a female to mate – permanently. After a while, the males become part of the female's body! They lose their fins, organs and ability to see. But they continue to help the female produce young.

Male anglerfish are attracted by the female's esca.

Biofluorescent Creatures

Fur that glows pink? Teeth, wings and beaks that give off green light? Is it science fiction? No!

Some creatures give off **fluorescent** (pronounced *floo-ress-ent*) light. This is known as **biofluorescence**. And, under special kinds of lights, we can see these creatures glow in the dark! Some reptiles, **amphibians**, birds, fish, **marsupials** and egg-laying mammals – such as the platypus – have this unique ability.

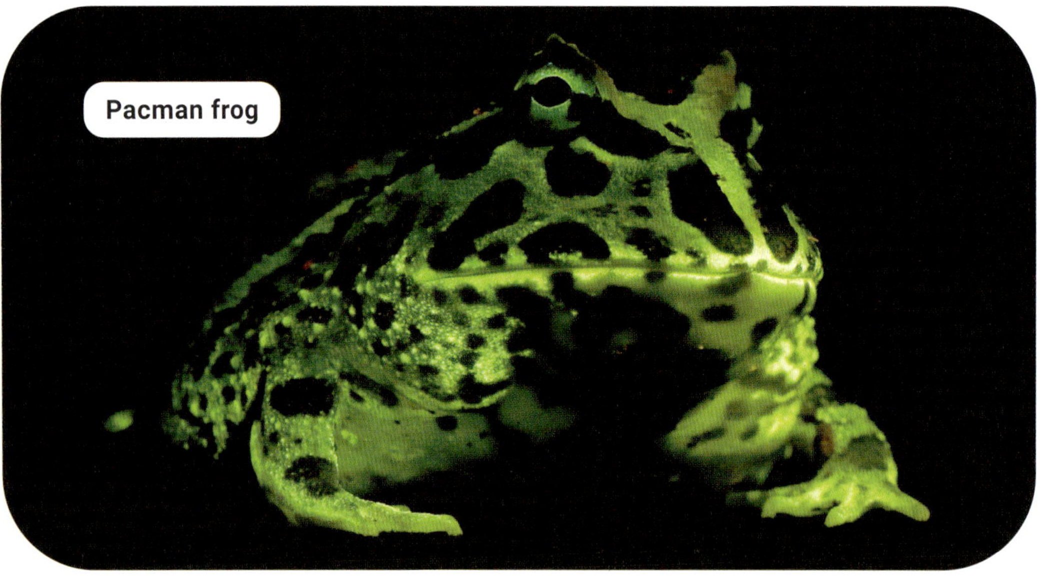

Pacman frog

Fluorescent light is produced when something absorbs a special type of light, found in sunlight: **ultraviolet (UV) light**. Humans usually can't see UV light. But when we shine a UV torch on a biofluorescent animal or plant, the animal or plant emits bright fluorescent shades of light that humans *can* see. Under a UV torch, the fur, beaks or skin of biofluorescent animals can reveal a pop of glowing colour. But without a UV torch, this colourful glow is invisible to humans.

Scientists don't know exactly why some animals are biofluorescent. It could help to protect the animals from predators, or it might help them to find each other in the dark.

Or, this ability to glow might be a strange natural accident, with no explanation at all.

Lots more research is needed.

crab spider

To See or Not to See: UV Light

Sunlight is made up of three kinds of light: visible light, infrared light (heat) and ultraviolet (UV) light. Most of the Sun's beams contain visible light and infrared light. UV light makes up a small part of the sunlight that reaches Earth.

UV light can cause sunburn and skin cancer. It can also turn corals white. Although humans can't see UV light, most other mammals can, as well as some birds, bees and other insects.

UV light from the Sun can damage coral, making it turn white.

Wombats

Wombats are marsupials, a type of mammal. They live in Australia and eat plants. Under natural lighting conditions, they look brown to humans.

But recently, scientists discovered something special. It all began with another unique Australian animal, the platypus. In 2020, US scientists shone a UV light on a platypus. The light revealed that the platypus's fur had dark-purple biofluorescence. Australian scientists checked this discovery by shining a UV light on another platypus. They, too, saw a dark purple glow! Then they shone the light on some wombats. The wombats' fur glowed blue-green! These experiments proved that wombats are biofluorescent.

wombat

Incredibly, many marsupials share this ability, including the echidna, bandicoot and bilby. But kangaroos do not.

A platypus glows dark purple under a UV light.

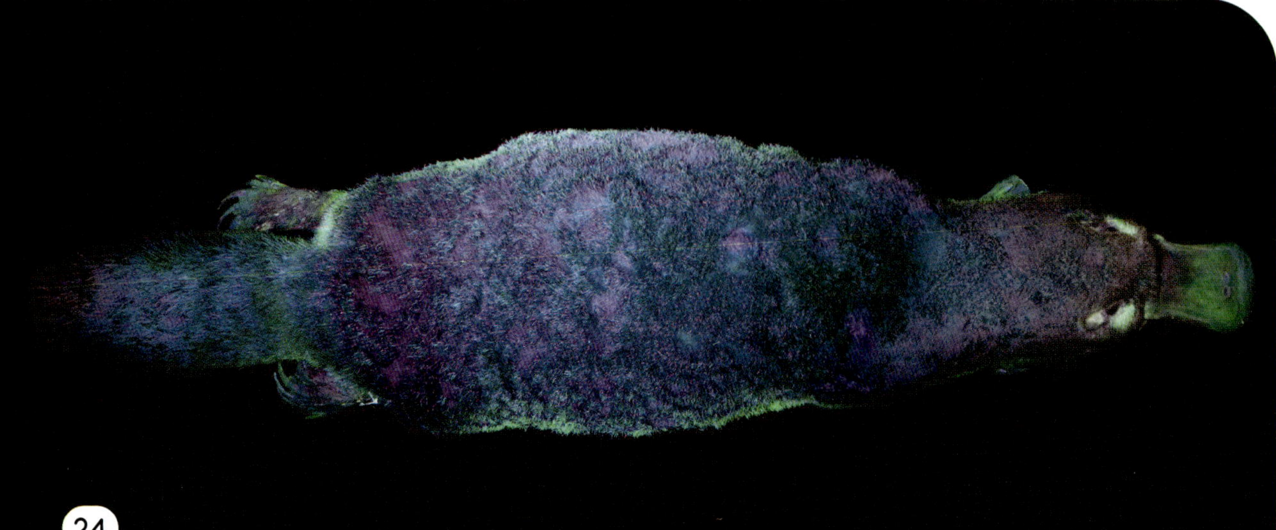

Wombat fur glows blue-green under a UV light.

Finding Friends

Wombats are nocturnal, meaning they sleep in the day and are active at night. They spend a lot of time alone, but when they want to find a mate, their ability to glow could make it easier to spot other wombats. Kangaroos also often sleep in the daytime, but they live in groups. They aren't biofluorescent, and scientists think that might be because they live so close to friends and family – they don't need to find them in the dark!

Flying Squirrels

You're most likely to spot a flying squirrel at night. They are native to North America, northern Europe and parts of Asia. These creatures can't really fly. Instead, they use their long arms, legs, fluffy tails and a strip of skin between their wrists and ankles to help them leap and glide as far as 90 metres from tree to tree.

In 2019, US scientists discovered that flying squirrels displayed hot-pink biofluorescence. That made these acrobatic creatures even more interesting. In 2021, researchers from Canada filmed some squirrels at night under UV lights. They recorded the squirrels' hot-pink glow, too.

Scientists don't know why flying squirrels have the ability to glow. On cold nights, squirrels from all different families snuggle together in cosy nests. The biofluorescence might be a way for flying squirrels to find their friends more easily in the dark. Or their pink glow could be a way to scare away night-time predators, such as raccoons. But perhaps it's a way to communicate something entirely different. Researchers are keen to find out more.

Flying squirrels are shaped so they can glide like a kite.

Sleepy Time

During the day, most types of squirrels are active, just like you. They search for nuts, seeds and berries. Because they sleep at night, they have no reason to glow in the dark. That ability would be wasted. But flying squirrels, unlike other squirrels, are nocturnal. And they are also biofluorescent! At night, it's easier for flying squirrels to find food, such as nuts, crickets, moths, grasshoppers, mice and mushrooms. Also, they can avoid hawks, snakes and other daytime predators.

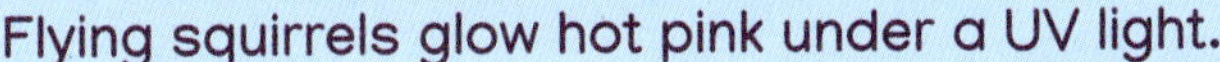

Flying squirrels glow hot pink under a UV light.

Hawksbill Sea Turtles

The ocean is home to a unique reptile. It's a biofluorescent sea turtle!

The hawksbill sea turtle's shell gives off a green or red glow in blue light.

In 2015, some scientists went diving in the ocean at night. They were researching biofluorescent coral in a coral reef. During the dive, they used torches that shone blue light. They were excited to see a hawksbill sea turtle, because they are very rare. But something else was even more exciting: the turtle gave off a fluorescent glow. Before this, scientists didn't know that a reptile could glow under certain kinds of light.

Remember how rainbows show us that sunlight bends and fans out into different colours in water? Well, underwater, out of all the different coloured beams of sunlight, blue light reaches the deepest (about 100 metres), giving everything a blue colour. Hawksbill sea turtles' shells absorb this blue light and emit a pale-green and red light.

Underwater, blue light reaches the deepest areas and often everything looks blue.

Whoa! Double Glow

The underside of a hawksbill sea turtle glows green, but its shell glows green and red. What's going on?

Some scientists think a type of algae could live on the shells and give off its own light. Others wonder if the hawksbill sea turtle can really glow in two colours.

It's tricky to study hawksbill sea turtles, since there are so few of them. But studying the similar, more common green sea turtle might help. If scientists can prove algae causes the red glow in green sea turtles, it's likely to be the same in the hawksbill.

A hawksbill sea turtle's shell glows green and red under blue light.

The turtle's biofluorescence has benefits. It may help it blend in with other light-emitting creatures, such as corals, fish and eels. This ability might help it to keep safe by hiding from predators.

Uncovering Light

Our world is full of natural sources of light. They are different and awe-inspiring. Simply by gazing out the window, you can experience sunlight or starlight – two examples of natural sources of light.

You can also discover things that use light in interesting and beautiful ways – like the Moon and the planets (reflection), and rainbows after a sun shower (reflection *and* refraction).

Depending on where you live or travel, you might be able to:

- glimpse a creature glowing in the dark
- visit a cave and spot glow-worms
- gaze upon a dark ocean and see light-emitting bacteria
- take a night-time walk and witness a light show of fireflies
- spot a glowing mushroom in the forest
- shine a special torch on the fur of wombats or flying squirrels to see their brilliant biofluorescent glow.

bioluminescence in the ocean

But many discoveries of biofluorescence are very new. The reasons some objects and living things give off light are still unclear. In time, scientists are sure to uncover a better understanding of glowing animals, just as they've continued to learn more about light in the universe and beyond.

Be curious and keep asking questions!

Glossary

amphibians *(noun)* — animals that spend an equal amount of time on land and in water

bacteria *(noun)* — tiny living things found in all natural environments

biofluorescence *(noun)* — the production of light by a living creature that has absorbed UV light

bioluminescence *(noun)* — the production of light by a living creature due to a chemical reaction in their bodies

chemical reaction *(noun)* — a process in which substances are changed into different substances

constellation *(noun)* — a group of stars in the night sky that make up a picture or a pattern

emit *(verb)* — to give off or let out something, e.g. light or heat

energy *(noun)* — the power that makes things move or work

fluorescent *(adjective)* — glowing brightly under a light

light beams *(noun)* — narrow lines of light that come from a light source

light pollution *(noun)* — when there is too much artificial light outside

lure *(noun)* — something used to encourage fish to attach themselves to a hook

marsupials *(noun)* — mammals that carry their babies in their pouches

mate *(noun)* — one of a pair of animals that breed and care for babies together

Moon phase *(noun)* — the shape of the Moon's sunlit portion as seen from Earth

mucus *(noun)* — a sticky substance created by living creatures

organ *(noun)* — a part of the body, like the heart or the brain

proteins *(noun)* — substances animals and humans need to help them grow and stay healthy

refraction *(noun)* — the bending of light

sources *(noun)* — the place something comes from

ultraviolet (UV) light *(noun)* — a kind of light from the Sun that humans can't see

Index